20TH-CENTURY
AMERICAN
POETRY

AN ANTHOLOGY

WRITERS' VOICES

SIGNAL HILL

WRITERS' VOICES™ was made possible by grants from: An anonymous foundation; The Vincent Astor Foundation; Booth Ferris Foundation; Exxon Corporation; James Money Management, Inc.; Knight Foundation; Philip Morris Companies Inc.; Scripps Howard Foundation; The House of Seagram; and the H.W. Wilson Foundation.

• • •

ATTENTION READERS: We would like to hear what you think about our books. Please send your comments or suggestions to:

The Editors
New Readers Press
P.O. Box 131
Syracuse, NY 13210-0131

• • •

Selections: ROBERT BLY. "To Live," "Thinking of 'Seclusion'," "After a Day of Work," "Driving to My Parents Home at Christmas" and "The Fallen Tree" from THIS TREE WILL BE HERE FOR A THOUSAND YEARS by Robert Bly © 1979 by Robert Bly. Reprinted by permission of HarperCollins Publishers Inc. "Snowbanks North of the House" from THE MAN IN THE BLACK COAT TURNS by Robert Bly. Reprinted by permission of Doubleday, a division of Bantam Doubleday Dell Publishing Group, Inc.

LUCILLE CLIFTON. "listen children," "breaklight," and "the thirty-eighth year" copyright © 1987 by Lucille Clifton. Reprinted from GOOD WOMAN POEMS AND A MEMOIR 1969–1989 by Lucille Clifton with the permission of BOA Editions, Brockport, NY.

ROBERT FROST. "The Road Not Taken," "Out, Out—," "Fire and Ice," "Dust of Snow," and "Stopping by Woods on a Snowy Evening" from THE POETRY OF ROBERT FROST edited by Edward Connery Lathem. Copyright 1916, 1923, © 1969 by Holt, Rinehart and Winston. Copyright 1944, 1951 by Robert Frost. Permission to reprint granted by Henry Holt and Company, Inc.

NIKKI GIOVANNI. "Nikki Rosa" and "Knoxville, Tennessee" from BLACK FEELINGS, BLACK TALK, BLACK JUDGMENT by Nikki Giovanni. © 1968, 1970 by Nikki Giovanni. Reprinted by permission of William Morrow & Co., Inc. "Revolutionary Dreams" from THE WOMEN AND THE MEN by Nikki Giovanni. © 1970, 1974, 1975 by Nikki Giovanni. Reprinted by permission of William Morrow & Co., Inc. "Poem for Carol" from MY HOUSE by Nikki Giovanni. © 1972 by Nikki Giovanni. Reprinted by permission of William Morrow & Co., Inc.

JOY HARJO. "She Had Some Horses" and "The Friday Before the Long Weekend" from SHE HAD SOME HORSES by Joy Harjo. Copyright © 1983 by Thunder's Mouth Press. Used by permission of the publisher, Thunder's Mouth Press.

(The following page is an extension of the copyright page.)

SIGNAL HILL®

Additional material
© 1991 Signal Hill Publications
A publishing imprint of Laubach Literacy International

10 9 8 7 6 5 4 3 2

ISBN 1-929631-29-3

First printing: March 1991

The words "Writers' Voices" are a trademark of New Readers Press.

Cover design: Paul Davis Studio
Text: Barbara Huntley

PRINTED WITH
SOY INK™

This book was printed on 100% recycled paper which contains 50% post-consumer waste.

Acknowledgments

We gratefully acknowledge the generous support of the following foundations and corporations that made the publication of WRITERS' VOICES and NEW WRITERS' VOICES possible: An anonymous foundation; The Vincent Astor Foundation; Booth Ferris Foundation; Exxon Corporation; James Money Management, Inc.; Knight Foundation; Philip Morris Companies Inc.; Scripps Howard Foundation; The House of Seagram; and the H.W. Wilson Foundation.

This book could not have been realized without the generous cooperation of the following authors and publishers: Robert Bly and his publishers, HarperCollins Publishers Inc. and Doubleday; Lucille Clifton and her publisher BOA Editions; Henry Holt and Company, the publisher of Robert Frost; Nikki Giovanni and her publisher William Morrow & Co.; Joy Harjo and her publisher Thunder's Mouth Press; Alfred A. Knopf, Inc., the publisher of Langston Hughes; HarperCollins Publishers Inc., the publisher of Edna St. Vincent Millay; and New Directions Publishing Corporation, the publisher of William Carlos Williams.

We deeply appreciate the contributions of the following suppliers: Cam Steel Die Rule Works Inc. (steel cutting die for display); Canadian Pacific Forest Products Ltd. (text stock); ComCom (text typesetting); Horizon Paper Co., Inc. and Domtar Fine Papers (cover stock); MCUSA (display header); Delta Corrugated Container (corrugated display); Phototype Color Graphics (cover color separations); and Arcata Graphics Company/Buffalo (cover and text printing and binding).

Our thanks to Paul Davis Studio, Barbara Huntley, and Ron Bel Bruno.

CONTENTS

NOTE TO THE READER

Poetry is a special form of writing. People enjoy reading poetry for both its sound and its meaning. Poetry is meant to be read both aloud and silently. It is meant to be read over and over and discussed with other readers. Reading poetry can be a deeply personal experience and a shared experience.

Every writer has a special voice. That is why we call our series *Writers' Voices*. We have chosen the poets in SELECTED FROM 20TH-CENTURY AMERICAN POETRY because each poet's special voice can be clearly heard. Some of them write about memories, some about nature, some about love and family—each in his or her special voice. We chose 20th-century poets so that you could learn what poets in recent years have chosen to write about and how they have chosen to write it. We chose American poets because we thought the way they use the English language might inspire you in your own writing.

Reading "Introduction to Poetry" will help you begin thinking about the poems you will read later in the book.

Eight poets are included in this book. There is an introduction to each poet and his or her poetry before the actual poems. Many readers enjoy finding out about the person who wrote the poems. Sometimes this information will give you more insight into the poetry.

If you are a new reader, you may want to have this book read aloud to you, perhaps more than once. Even if you are a more experienced reader, you may enjoy hearing the poems read aloud before reading them silently to yourself. Reading aloud is one of the special pleasures of poetry.

We encourage you to read *actively*. Here are some things you can do.

Before Reading

• Read the front and back covers of the book and look at the cover illustration. Ask yourself what you expect the book to be about.

• Think about why you want to read this book. Perhaps you are interested in writing poetry yourself.

• Look at the Contents page. Decide which poets and poetry you want to read and in what order.

During Reading

● There may be words that are difficult to read. Keep reading to see if the meaning becomes clear. If it doesn't, go back and reread the difficult part or discuss it with others. Or look up the words in a dictionary.

● Ask yourself questions as you read. For example: What does this poem mean? Does it mean more than one thing?

After Reading

● Think about what you have read. Did you identify with what the poet was trying to say? Did the poem make you see any of your own experiences in a new light?

● Talk with others about your thoughts.

The editors of *Writers' Voices* hope you will write to us. We want to know your thoughts about our books.

INTRODUCTION TO POETRY

What Is Poetry?

Most of us know a poem when we see one. The shape of a poem is the first thing we notice, because poems have a special form or structure.

The first time we read a poem, we notice that it has a special rhythm or beat. At first, we may not be aware just what about the poem is making us feel the rhythm. We just know it is there.

The first time we read a poem, we may form an opinion about what the poet means to say. But when we read the poem over and over again, each time we may find new meanings in the poet's words. The poet uses words very carefully and in very special ways to convey meaning. This careful use of language to create many levels of meaning is an important part of what makes poetry special.

Structure, Rhythm, Language and Meaning

The first poems may have been prayers to the gods, spoken by ancient peoples. They may have chanted them aloud to music. These people also used special language to make these prayers sound different from ordinary conversation.

Before the invention of pencils and paper, older people would tell their history and beliefs to their children. To remember these stories, people told them in rhyme.

Once people could write down these stories, they wrote them in lines with the rhyming word at the end of the line. The lines were short so the story and rhyme would stand out. Compactness became one of the marks of poetry.

Song had a great influence on the development of poetry. These stories were often put to music and the lines were written to go with the rhythms of the music.

People also wrote songs about thoughts and feelings. The songwriters chose the words for these songs carefully to express the beauty and depth of their emotions.

Poetry became a separate form of writing. It had a special structure, rhythm and language. Poems use language to express beautiful or imaginative or deeply felt thoughts and emotions. They may also use images to express ideas and emotions. For example, look at Lucille Clifton's poetry. She chooses images to describe herself, such as "plain as bread" or "round as a cake."

Now poets write poetry for its own sake. They concentrate on how best to express their thoughts and feelings. Their words and images are deep and rich, creating many levels of meaning.

Over time, the structure of poems has changed. Poets experiment with different ways of shaping their poems. For example, many poets no longer use rhyme at all. And many poets use lines of different lengths in the same poem.

Poetry is the "bare bones" of writing, conveying many levels of meaning in the fewest possible, but most carefully chosen, words.

Reading a Poem

When you start to read a poem, look at how the poet has shaped the poem. This will provide you with many clues on how to read and understand the poem.

Each poet chooses the form that best reflects the emotion and meanings he or she wants to convey. The length of the lines and where each one breaks often have nothing to do with where the sentences end. Instead, they are broken according to how they should be read. Some poets do not use capital letters or punctuation. Some use a lot of white space between the lines or parts of their poem.

Where a poet leaves a white space, you should pause for a moment in your reading. The poet John Ciardi called these pauses "the silences."

Listen for the rhythm of the poem as you read. The poet may create this rhythm in many ways. It may come from the number of syllables or sounds in each line (the "meter" of the poem). It may come from the rhymes at the ends of lines. Or it may come from rhymes within the lines of poetry. The rhythm may come from the repetition of certain words or phrases. Or it may come from echoing certain word sounds in different words. The rhythm will also be affected by the poem's silences.

The rhythm of the poem will also give you clues as to the poem's meanings. Look at Joy Harjo's poem "She Had Some Horses"; notice the rhythm she has chosen and how it affects the poem.

Look carefully at the poet's language. Poets choose words that best capture their emotion and meanings.

After you have read the poem, think about its meanings. Then go back and reread it. Look deeper into the poem. What is the poet saying beneath the surface meaning of the poem? John

Ciardi says, "The poetic structure *releases* its 'meaning'; it does not *say* it."

Hearing a Poem

Poems are not meant just to be read, they are also meant to be heard. When you hear a poem read aloud, you will get a new and different feeling for it.

Read the poem out loud to yourself or to others or have it read to you. What is different when you hear it rather than when you read it silently?

Discussing Poetry

Discuss poems you have read with people who have read the same poems. Most people will be able to agree about what the surface meaning of a poem is. But each person may have a different opinion on what else the poet is saying.

Readers identify with poets in a deeply emotional and very personal way. Readers often read a poem and say, "Yes, I have felt that too." And yet, each reader may be responding to a different feeling, a different meaning.

The Poets in This Book

You do not have to read all the poets in this book, nor do you have to read them in any particular order.

These eight poets have been selected to illustrate the many paths that poetry can take. They will show you that, like people, no two poems are alike. And they will show you the many ways that poetry expresses the deepest emotions and ideas that we all share.

Writing Poetry

When you have a feeling or idea that moves you, respect its right to be heard as a poem and let it emerge on paper. Experiment with different forms, different rhythms, different language. And when the right shape and rhythm and language for your poem comes along, trust that you will hear it.

ROBERT FROST

Robert Frost was born in 1874 in San Francisco, California. After his father's death in 1885, his mother followed her husband's instructions and buried him in Lawrence, Massachusetts. She and her two children remained in the East.

Frost attended high school in Lawrence where he began to be known as a poet. His high grades put him at the top of his class. But when he graduated, he shared the top honors with a girl, Elinor White, whose grades were even better than his own. In 1895, they were married.

A few years later, the Frosts moved to a farm in Derry, New Hampshire. It was here that the five Frost children were born (one died as an infant). Money was tight and life was difficult. But Frost got a teaching job and kept writing.

Frost often said that he had three occupations in life: teaching, farming and poetry. There was never any doubt that poetry came first. Yet life on the farm provided Frost with the themes he used in his poetry: rural life and work, nature and the seasons.

In 1912, Frost moved his family to England. There his first and second books of poetry were published and he received the recognition he had not found in America. When World War I broke out in Europe, he was forced to return to America in 1915.

Now it was easier for Frost to find a publisher for his poetry. As his poetry became known, he was asked to teach and speak at many colleges. Two of his books won the Pulitzer Prize (an important literary prize). Frost won many honors and became the most recognized poet in America. He died in 1963.

Frost's poetry is mostly written in the first person—from the poet's point of view. His poems have the tight form of traditional poetry but they sound like the voice of a living person. The voice seems simple and down-to-earth yet also wise.

Frost has said, "Poetry provides the one permissible way of saying one thing and meaning another." He describes real country scenes in his poetry. Yet when you think about the scenes, there are other deeper meanings.

❧ *The Road Not Taken* ❧
~1915~

Two roads diverged in a yellow wood,
And sorry I could not travel both
And be one traveler, long I stood
And looked down one as far as I could
To where it bent in the undergrowth;

Then took the other, as just as fair,
And having perhaps the better claim,
Because it was grassy and wanted wear;
Though as for that, the passing there
Had worn them really about the same,

And both that morning equally lay
In leaves no step had trodden black.
Oh, I kept the first for another day!
Yet knowing how way leads on to way,
I doubted if I should ever come back.

I shall be telling this with a sigh
Somewhere ages and ages hence:
Two roads diverged in a wood, and I—
I took the one less traveled by,
And that has made all the difference.

❧ *"Out, Out—"* ❧
～ 1 9 1 6 ～

The buzz saw snarled and rattled in the yard
And made dust and dropped stove-length sticks
of wood,
Sweet-scented stuff when the breeze drew
across it.
And from there those that lifted eyes
could count
Five mountain ranges one behind the other
Under the sunset far into Vermont.
And the saw snarled and rattled, snarled
and rattled,
As it ran light, or had to bear a load.
And nothing happened: day was all but done.
Call it a day, I wish they might have said
To please the boy by giving him the half hour
That a boy counts so much when saved
from work.
His sister stood beside them in her apron
To tell them "Supper." At the word, the saw,
As if to prove saws knew what supper meant,
Leaped out at the boy's hand, or seemed
to leap—
He must have given the hand. However it was,
Neither refused the meeting. But the hand!
The boy's first outcry was a rueful laugh,
As he swung toward them holding up the hand,

Half in appeal, but half as if to keep
The life from spilling. Then the boy saw all—
Since he was old enough to know, big boy
Doing a man's work, though a child at heart—
He saw all spoiled. "Don't let him cut
                    my hand off—
The doctor, when he comes. Don't let him,
                         sister!"
So. But the hand was gone already.
The doctor put him in the dark of ether.
He lay and puffed his lips out with his breath.
And then—the watcher at his pulse took fright.
No one believed. They listened at his heart.
Little—less—nothing!—and that ended it.
No more to build on there. And they, since they
Were not the one dead, turned to their affairs.

❧ Dust of Snow ❧
~1920~

The way a crow
Shook down on me
The dust of snow
From a hemlock tree

Has given my heart
A change of mood
And saved some part
Of a day I had rued.

❧ *Fire and Ice* ❧
～ 1 9 2 0 ～

Some say the world will end in fire,
Some say in ice.
From what I've tasted of desire
I hold with those who favor fire.
But if it had to perish twice,
I think I know enough of hate
To say that for destruction ice
Is also great
And would suffice.

❧ Stopping by Woods ❧ On a Snowy Evening

～ 1 9 2 3 ～

Whose woods these are I think I know.
His house is in the village, though;
He will not see me stopping here
To watch his woods fill up with snow.

My little horse must think it queer
To stop without a farmhouse near
Between the woods and frozen lake
The darkest evening of the year.

He gives his harness bells a shake
To ask if there is some mistake.
The only other sound's the sweep
Of easy wind and downy flake.

The woods are lovely, dark, and deep,
But I have promises to keep,
And miles to go before I sleep,
And miles to go before I sleep.

WILLIAM CARLOS WILLIAMS

William Carlos Williams was born in 1883 in Rutherford, New Jersey. He went to school in both the United States and Europe. His first book of poems was published in 1909 while he was completing his studies to become a doctor. He set up his medical practice in Rutherford, married and had two sons.

In between seeing patients, Williams jotted down quick, concise images of life he saw around himself. Sometimes he wrote them on prescription pads. He called them "snapshots."

Williams had strong ideas about both America and poetry. He believed that his poetry should represent the American language and culture. He wrote about everyday objects and ordinary people—and he wrote about them in words that people used every day and could understand.

Williams wanted to talk directly to his readers. He took simple things and described them in simple words so the reader could see to the heart of the experience or event he was describing.

In order to achieve his goals, Williams had

to invent new ways to write poetry. He freed his poetry from the traditional forms and language. He made it live word by word and line by line in new shapes and sounds.

Williams lived in Rutherford until his death in 1963. He never wanted to be considered an "artist" in the sense of a person different from others. But his talents were widely recognized and he influenced many younger poets. He won the Pulitzer Prize in 1963.

❧ *The Red Wheelbarrow* ❧
⌒ 1 9 2 3 ⌒

so much depends
upon

a red wheel
barrow

glazed with rain
water

beside the white
chickens.

 23

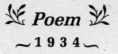

Poem

~ 1 9 3 4 ~

As the cat
climbed over
the top of

the jamcloset
first the right
forefoot

carefully
then the hind
stepped down

into the pit of
the empty
flowerpot

This Is Just to Say

~ 1 9 3 4 ~

I have eaten
the plums
that were in
the icebox

and which
you were probably

saving
for breakfast

Forgive me
they were delicious
so sweet
and so cold

🌿 *To a Poor Old Woman* 🌿
～1 9 3 5～

munching a plum on
the street a paper bag
of them in her hand

They taste good to her
They taste good
to her. They taste
good to her

You can see it by
the way she gives herself
to the one half
sucked out in her hand

Comforted
a solace of ripe plums
seeming to fill the air
They taste good to her

🌿 The Last Words of 🌿 My English Grandmother

～ 1 9 3 8 ～

There were some dirty plates
and a glass of milk
beside her on a small table
near the rank, disheveled bed—

Wrinkled and nearly blind
she lay and snored
rousing with anger in her tones
to cry for food,

Gimme something to eat—
They're starving me—
I'm all right I won't go
to the hospital. No, no, no

Give me something to eat
Let me take you
to the hospital, I said
and after you are well

you can do as you please.
She smiled, Yes
you do what you please first
then I can do what I please—

Oh, oh, oh! she cried
as the ambulance men lifted
her to the stretcher—
Is this what you call

making me comfortable?
By now her mind was clear—
Oh you think you're smart
you young people,

she said, but I'll tell you
you don't know anything.
Then we started.
On the way

we passed a long row
of elms. She looked at them
awhile out of
the ambulance window and said,

What are all those
fuzzy-looking things out there?
Trees? Well, I'm tired
of them and rolled her head away.

EDNA ST. VINCENT MILLAY

Edna St. Vincent Millay was born in 1892 in Rockland, Maine. Her parents divorced when she was young. She lived with her mother and sister in Maine near the ocean and mountains.

Millay wrote her first poem when she was five years old. She regularly sent her poems to a children's magazine.

In 1917, Millay graduated from college and had her first book of poetry published. She moved to New York City where she made friends with many intellectual and artistic young people. She joined the Provincetown Players, a new and exciting theater group. She wrote three plays in verse for the group. She also acted in many of their plays.

By 1921, Millay had written three more books of poetry and verse. She decided to move to Europe for a writing holiday. When she returned two years later, she had a new book of poems titled *The Harp-Weaver and Other Poems* ready for publication. This book won her the Pulitzer Prize.

That same year, she also got married and moved with her husband to a farm in Massachusetts. She lived and wrote there until her death in 1950.

Millay was most famous for her lyrical poems, poems that pour out her thoughts and feelings like song. In these poems, she expresses her feelings about love, the experiences of life and the shadow of death in life.

Millay's poetry does not usually refer to a specific time or place. And since she shaped her poetry in many traditional forms, it could have been written at any time.

❧ *First Fig* ❧
～1920～

My candle burns at both ends;
  It will not last the night;
But ah, my foes, and oh, my friends—
  It gives a lovely light!

 Recuerdo
["Memory"]
～1 9 2 0～

We were very tired, we were very merry—
We had gone back and forth all night
                                on the ferry.
It was bare and bright, and smelled
                                like a stable—
But we looked into a fire, we leaned
                                across a table,
We lay on a hill-top underneath the moon;
And the whistles kept blowing,
                          and the dawn came soon.

We were very tired, we were very merry—
We had gone back and forth all night
                                on the ferry;
And you ate an apple, and I ate a pear,
From a dozen of each we had bought
                                somewhere;
And the sky went wan, and the wind
                                came cold,
And the sun rose dripping, a bucketful of gold.

We were very tired, we were very merry,
We had gone back and forth all night
                                on the ferry.
We hailed, "Good morrow, mother!"
                            to a shawl-covered head,

And bought a morning paper,
                    which neither of us read;
And she wept, "God bless you!"
                    for the apples and pears,
And we gave her all our money
                    but our subway fares.

🌿 Thursday 🌿

～1920～

And if I loved you Wednesday,
    Well, what is that to you?
I do not love you Thursday—
    So much is true.

And why you come complaining
    Is more than I can see.
I loved you Wednesday,—yes—but what
    Is that to me?

 Spring

~1921~

To what purpose, April, do you return again?
Beauty is not enough.
You can no longer quiet me with the redness
Of little leaves opening stickily.
I know what I know.
The sun is hot on my neck as I observe
The spikes of the crocus.
The smell of the earth is good.
It is apparent that there is no death.
But what does that signify?
Not only under ground are the brains of men
Eaten by maggots.
Life in itself
Is nothing,
An empty cup, a flight of uncarpeted stairs.
It is not enough that yearly, down this hill,
April
Comes like an idiot, babbling and
                        strewing flowers.

🌿 A Visit to the Asylum 🌿

～ 1 9 2 3 ～

Once from a big, big building,
When I was small, small,
The queer folk in the windows
Would smile at me and call.

And in the hard wee gardens
Such pleasant men would hoe:
"Sir, may we touch the little girl's hair!"—
It was so red, you know.

They cut me coloured asters
With shears so sharp and neat,
They brought me grapes and plums and pears
And pretty cakes to eat.

And out of all the windows,
No matter where we went,
The merriest eyes would follow me
And make me compliment.

There were a thousand windows,
All latticed up and down.
And up to all the windows,
When we went back to town,

The queer folk put their faces,
As gentle as could be;
"Come again, little girl!" they called, and I
Called back, "You come see me!"

LANGSTON HUGHES

Langston Hughes was born in 1902 in Joplin, Missouri. His parents divorced when he was young but he remained close to both of them.

As a boy, he lived in Kansas with his mother. There he discovered the joys of reading. Looking back, he wrote: "Then it was that books began to happen to me, and I began to believe in nothing but books and the wonderful world of books."

He also discovered the rich musical heritage of his African-American forebears. When he was 12, he attended a revival meeting where he was caught up in the music and the emotion. In his uncle's barbershop, he first heard the blues.

Hughes set out to write poetry in the spirit of jazz. He was the first poet to adapt the form and mood of blues to poetry. Many of his poems were set to music. His first book of poetry, published in 1926, was called *The Weary Blues.*

In his poetry, Hughes was interested in capturing many aspects of black life in the United States, both positive and negative. He also tried to show the connections between modern African-Americans and their roots. He speaks of sadness and happiness, of hopes and dreams and love. Hughes made a comment about the blues that could also apply to his poems: "The mood of the *Blues* is almost always despondency, but when they are sung people laugh."

Hughes died in 1967. During his life, he wrote 16 books of poems, two novels, three collections of short stories, 20 plays, eight children's books and 12 radio and television scripts.

❧ *The Negro Speaks of Rivers* ❧
～1 9 2 6 ～

I've known rivers:
I've known rivers ancient as the world and
   older than the flow of human blood
   in human veins.

My soul has grown deep like the rivers.

I bathed in the Euphrates when dawns
   were young.
I built my hut near the Congo and
   it lulled me to sleep.
I looked upon the Nile and
   raised the pyramids above it.

I heard the singing of the Mississippi when
  Abe Lincoln went down to New Orleans,
and I've seen its muddy bosom
  turn all golden in the sunset.

I've known rivers:
Ancient, dusky rivers.

My soul has grown deep like the rivers.

❧ Dreams ❧
～1 9 3 2～

Hold fast to dreams
For if dreams die
Life is a broken-winged bird
That cannot fly.

Hold fast to dreams
For when dreams go
Life is a barren field
Frozen with snow.

🌿 Aunt Sue's Stories 🌿
~Collected 1959~

Aunt Sue has a head full of stories.
Aunt Sue has a whole heart full of stories.
Summer nights on the front porch
Aunt Sue cuddles a brown-faced child
                                   to her bosom
And tells him stories.
Black slaves
Working in the hot sun,
And black slaves
Walking in the dewy night,
And black slaves
Singing sorrow songs on the banks
                        of a mighty river
Mingle themselves softly
In the flow of old Aunt Sue's voice,
Mingle themselves softly
In the dark shadows that cross and recross
Aunt Sue's stories.

And the dark-faced child, listening,
Knows that Aunt Sue's stories are
                              real stories.
He knows that Aunt Sue never got
                            her stories
Out of any book at all,
But that they came
Right out of her own life.

The dark-faced child is quiet
Of a summer night
Listening to Aunt Sue's stories.

❧ *As Befits a Man* ❧
～C o l l e c t e d 1 9 5 9～

I don't mind dying—
But I'd hate to die all alone!
I want a dozen pretty women
To holler, cry, and moan.

I don't mind dying
But I want my funeral to be fine:
A row of long tall mamas
Fainting, fanning, and crying.

I want a fish-tail hearse
And sixteen fish-tail cars,
A big brass band
And a whole truck load of flowers.

When they let me down,
Down into the clay,
I want the women to holler:
Please don't take him away!
          Ow-ooo-oo-o!
Don't take daddy away!

🌿 *Harlem Night Song* 🌿

~Collected 1959~

Come,
Let us roam the night together
Singing.

I love you.

Across
The Harlem roof-tops
Moon is shining.
Night sky is blue.
Stars are great drops
Of golden dew.

Down the street
A band is playing.

I love you.

Come,
Let us roam the night together
Singing.

❧ *Daybreak in Alabama* ❧
⁓ C o l l e c t e d   1 9 5 9 ⁓

When I get to be a composer
I'm gonna write me some music about
Daybreak in Alabama
And I'm gonna put the purtiest songs in it
Rising out of the ground like a swamp mist
And falling out of heaven like soft dew.
I'm gonna put some tall tall trees in it
And the scent of pine needles
And the smell of red clay after rain
And long red necks
And poppy colored faces
And big brown arms
And the field daisy eyes
Of black and white black white black
*   people*
And I'm gonna put white hands
And black hands and brown and yellow
*   hands*
And red clay earth hands in it
Touching everybody with kind fingers
And touching each other natural as dew
In that dawn of music when I
Get to be a composer
And write about daybreak
In Alabama.

ROBERT BLY

Robert Bly was born in 1926 in Madison, Minnesota. He served in the navy during the Second World War. In 1950, he graduated from college and lived in New York City for several years. He then went to Norway for a year to visit the land of his ancestors.

In 1955, Bly married and moved back to a farm in Minnesota. His first book of poems, *Silence in the Snowy Fields*, was published in 1962.

Bly writes poetry about the Minnesota landscapes he loves. He describes these scenes in a straightforward way, yet he also seeks to show things we cannot see. He tries to capture the invisible core of this natural world. He also reveals the "landscape" of his own mind as he experiences an event.

In this way, Bly expresses the special vision of a poet. The poet lives in and observes the real world but also lives in the world of his mind and imagination. He must write out of his experiences in both worlds.

Bly takes an image we might all recognize, such as a farm or driving a car, and adds meaning to it. In this way, he gives us insight into the mysteries of nature.

In the late 1960s and early 1970s, Bly took a strong stand against the Vietnam War. His book of antiwar poems won the National Book Award in 1968.

Today Bly spends a part of each year visiting colleges and literary clubs. He reads his poems and plays the dulcimer. These readings have shown many people that poetry can have importance in their lives. Bly has especially made them think about how nature relates to their lives.

🌿 *To Live* 🌿
~ 1 9 7 9 ~

"Living" means eating up particles of death,
 as a child picks up crumbs
 from around the table.
"Floating" means letting the crumbs
 fall behind you on the path.
To live is to rush ahead eating up
 your own death, like an endgate,
 open, hurrying into night.

🌿 *Driving My Parents* 🌿
Home at Christmas
～1979～

As I drive my parents home through the snow,
their frailty hesitates on the edge
   of a mountainside.
I call over the cliff,
only snow answers.
They talk quietly
of hauling water, of eating an orange,
of a grandchild's photograph
   left behind last night.
When they open the door of their house,
   they disappear.
And the oak when it falls in the forest
   who hears it through miles and miles
   of silence?
They sit so close to each other . . .
   as if pressed together by the snow.

🌿 Thinking of "Seclusion" 🌿
～ 1 9 7 9 ～

I get up late and ask what has to be
  done today.
Nothing has to be done, so the farm looks
  doubly good.
The blowing maple leaves fit so well
  with the moving grass.
The shadow of my writing shack looks small
  beside the growing trees.

Never be with your children, let them get
  stringy like radishes!
Let your wife worry about the lack of money!
Your whole life is like some drunkard's dream!
You haven't combed your hair
  for a whole month!

🌿 After a Day of Work 🌿
～ 1 9 7 9 ～

How lightly the legs walk over
  the snow-whitened fields!
I wander far off, like a daddy-longlegs
  blown over the water.
All day I worked alone, hour after hour.
It is January, easy walking, the big snows
  still to come.

🌿 The Fallen Tree 🌿
~ 1 9 7 9 ~

After a long walk I come down to the shore.
A cottonwood tree lies stretched out
  in the grass.
This tree knocked down by lightning—
and a hollow the owls made open now
  to the rain.
Disasters are all right, if they teach
  men and women
to turn their hollow places up.

The tree lies stretched out
  where it fell in the grass.
It is so mysterious, waters below, waters
  above,
so little of it we can ever know!

🌿 Snowbanks North 🌿
Of the House
~ 1 9 8 3 ~

Those great sweeps of snow that stop
  suddenly six feet from the house . . .
Thoughts that go so far.
The boy gets out of high school
  and reads no more books;
the son stops calling home.

The mother puts down her rolling pin
  and makes no more bread.
And the wife looks at her husband one night
  at a party, and loves him no more.
The energy leaves the wine,
  and the minister falls leaving the church.
It will not come closer—
the one inside moves back, and the hands
  touch nothing, and are safe.

The father grieves for his son,
  and will not leave the room
  where the coffin stands.
He turns away from his wife,
  and she sleeps alone.

And the sea lifts and falls all night,
  the moon goes on
  through the unattached heavens alone.

The toe of the shoe pivots
in the dust . . .
And the man in the black coat turns,
  and goes back down the hill.
No one knows why he came,
  or why he turned away,
  and did not climb the hill.

LUCILLE CLIFTON

Lucille Sayles Clifton was born in 1936 in Depew, New York. At age 16, she left home for the first time to attend Howard University in Washington, D.C. She later transferred to Fredonia State Teachers College in New York State.

After college, she married Fred Clifton. They had four daughters and two sons.

Family is the most important theme in Clifton's poetry. She implies that only through families can we find a true sense of ourselves and how we fit into the larger world. She also suggests that even though family relationships can cause pain, they can also heal.

Clifton is also interested in her African-American heritage. She writes of her roots in Africa and of her family's history in the United States. She tells the struggles of blacks in slavery and in today's inner cities. She also has written a series of poems about famous African-Americans including Eldridge Cleaver, Angela Davis and Little Richard.

Religion also plays a part in Clifton's poetry. She writes about religion as part of everyday life. She has written a series of poems based on characters in the Bible.

Clifton's first book, *Good Times*, was published in 1969. In this book and in all her subsequent work, she focuses on the grief and laughter we experience in families and in life.

Clifton teaches at the University of California at Santa Cruz. She says of herself, "I am a black woman poet, and I write like one."

~ 1 9 7 2 ~

listen children
keep this in the place
you have for keeping
always
keep it all ways

we have never hated black

listen
we have been ashamed
hopeless   tired   mad
but always
all ways
we loved us

we have always loved each other
children   all ways

pass it on

🌿 *breaklight* 🌿
~1974~

light keeps on breaking.
i keep knowing
the language of other nations.
i keep hearing
tree talk
water words
and i keep knowing what they mean.
and light just keeps on breaking.
last night
the fears of my mother came
knocking and when i
opened the door
they tried to explain themselves
and i understood
everything they said.

🌿 🌿
~1974~

the thirty eighth year
of my life,
plain as bread
round as a cake
an ordinary woman.

an ordinary woman.

i had expected to be
smaller than this,
more beautiful,
wiser in afrikan ways,
more confident,
i had expected
more than this.

i will be forty soon.
my mother once was forty.

my mother died at forty four,
a woman of sad countenance
leaving behind a girl
awkward as a stork.
my mother was thick,
her hair was a jungle and
she was very wise
and beautiful
and sad.

i have dreamed dreams
for you mama
more than once.
i have wrapped me
in your skin
and made you live again
more than once.
i have taken the bones you hardened
and built daughters

and they blossom and promise fruit
like afrikan trees.
i am a woman now.
an ordinary woman.

in the thirty eighth
year of my life,
surrounded by life,
a perfect picture of
blackness blessed,
i had not expected this
loneliness.

if it is western,
if it is the final
europe in my mind,
if in the middle of my life
i am turning the final turn
into the shining dark
let me come to it whole
and holy
not afraid
not lonely
out of my mother's life
into my own.
into my own.

i had expected more than this.
i had not expected to be
an ordinary woman.

NIKKI GIOVANNI

Yolande Cornelia (Nikki) Giovanni was born in 1943 in Knoxville, Tennessee.

While she was at Fisk University in the 1960s, Giovanni became involved with civil rights issues. Across the United States, young African-Americans were discovering their heritage and laying claim to it. Black pride and black power were the goals they pursued.

Her first book of poetry, *Black Feeling, Black Talk*, was published in 1968. She started her own publishing cooperative to produce her second book, *Black Judgement*, in 1970. She also produced a record album, *Truth Is on Its Way*, which sold over 100,000 copies.

The poems and the record spoke directly to the feelings of her peers. She wrote about who and what she was. She explored what it meant to be black. She wrote about her black past and how it related to her present.

Soon Giovanni was invited to read her poetry on college campuses across the country. She was a voice for her generation.

Giovanni's other main theme is expressed by her belief that family is love and love is family. She has faith in her parents, herself and her son. Her hope for the future of the black community is based on the family.

During the early 1970s, Giovanni became well known for her down-to-earth readings. She became more vocal in describing black America to black Americans. But by 1975, she began to bring a softer quality to her work.

Giovanni is an advocate for individual independence. She believes each person should search for his or her own values and identity within the black community.

Of her work, she has said, "The purpose of poetry has to be the idea, the communicating, the reaching over the edge."

Knoxville, Tennessee
~ 1 9 6 8 ~

I always like summer
best
you can eat fresh corn
from daddy's garden
and okra
and greens
and cabbage
and lots of
barbecue
and buttermilk

and homemade ice-cream
at the church picnic
and listen to
gospel music
outside
at the church
homecoming
and go to the mountains with
your grandmother
and go barefooted
and be warm
all the time
not only when you go to bed
and sleep

❧ Nikki-Rosa ❧
～ 1 9 6 8 ～

childhood remembrances are always a drag
if you're Black
you always remember things like living
                              in Woodlawn
with no inside toilet
and if you become famous or something
they never talk about how happy you were
                                    to have
your mother
all to yourself and

how good the water felt when you got
                              your bath
from one of those
big tubs that folk in chicago barbecue in
and somehow when you talk about home
it never gets across how much you
understood their feelings
as the whole family attended meetings
                              about Hollydale
and even though you remember
your biographers never understand
your father's pain as he sells his stock
and another dream goes
And though you're poor it isn't poverty that
concerns you
and though they fought a lot
it isn't your father's drinking
                              that makes any difference
but only that everybody is together and you
and your sister have happy birthdays and
                              very good Christmasses
and I really hope no white person ever
                              has cause
to write about me
because they never understand
Black love is Black wealth and they'll
probably talk about my hard childhood
and never understand that
all the while I was quite happy

🌿 *A Poem for Carol* 🌿
(May She Always Wear Red Ribbons)
~ **1971** ~

when i was very little
though it's still true today
there were no sidewalks in lincoln heights
and the home we had on jackson street
was right next to a bus stop and a sewer
which didn't really ever become offensive
but one day from the sewer a little kitten
with one eye gone
came crawling out
though she never really came into our
                              yard but just
sort of hung by to watch the folk
my sister who was always softhearted
                              but able
to act effectively started taking milk
out to her while our father would only say
don't bring him home and everyday
after school i would rush home to see
                              if she was still
there and if gary had fed her but I could
                              never
bring myself to go near her
she was so loving
and so hurt and so singularly beautiful and
                              i knew

i had nothing to give that would
replace her one gone eye

and if i had named her which i didn't i'm
sure
i would have called her carol

Revolutionary Dreams

1975

i used to dream militant
dreams of taking
over america to show
these white folks how it should be
done
i used to dream radical dreams
of blowing everyone away with
my perceptive powers
of correct analysis
i even used to think i'd be the one
to stop the riot and negotiate the
peace
then i awoke and dug
that if i dreamed natural
dreams of being a natural
woman doing what a woman
does when she's natural
i would have a revolution

JOY HARJO

Joy Harjo was born in 1951 in Tulsa, Oklahoma. Her parents were Creek Indians. When they divorced, Harjo was sent to a boarding school run by the Bureau of Indian Affairs. The school emphasized education through the arts. Harjo concentrated on painting.

Harjo went on to the Institute of American Indian Arts, a high school for Native Americans. She continued painting there and also wrote lyrics for an acid rock band.

At the University of New Mexico, Harjo began taking writing classes and became interested in poetry. Finally, she felt she had to choose between painting and writing. She says she chose writing because "for me, it was the harder thing to do."

Harjo explores her Native American heritage and her own relationship to these roots. Harjo writes about pride and traditions that have survived from generation to generation.

Harjo says, "We carry the land with us." And the land is a major element in Harjo's poetry. Her first book of poetry was *She Had Some Horses*, published in 1983. The unique landscape of the American Southwest is important to the images Harjo creates. The horse is a part of this landscape. For Harjo, the horse is a strong symbol of both tradition and today's reality.

Harjo is also concerned with the loss of Native American culture. She writes about what has resulted from historical efforts to deprive many Native Americans of their identity.

Other poems explore the many sides of love and intimacy.

In 1990, Harjo won an American Indian Distinguished Achievement Award. She teaches creative writing and Native American studies at the University of Arizona in Tucson.

❦ *She Had Some Horses* ❦
~ 1 9 8 3 ~

She had some horses.

She had horses who were bodies of sand.
She had horses who were maps drawn of blood.
She had horses who were skins of ocean water.
She had horses who were the blue air of sky.
She had horses who were fur and teeth.
She had horses who were clay and would break.
She had horses who were splintered red cliff.

She had some horses.

She had horses with long, pointed breasts.

She had horses with full, brown thighs.
She had horses who laughed too much.
She had horses who threw rocks at glass houses
She had horses who licked razor blades.

She had some horses.

She had horses who danced
in their mothers' arms.
She had horses who thought they were the sun
and their bodies shone and burned like stars.
She had horses who waltzed nightly on the moo
She had horses who were much too shy,
and kept quiet in stalls of their own making.

She had some horses.

She had horses who liked Creek Stomp
Dance songs.
She had horses who cried in their beer.
She had horses who spit at male queens
who made them afraid of themselves.
She had horses who said they weren't afraid.
She had horses who lied.
She had horses who told the truth,
who were stripped bare of their tongues.

She had some horses.

She had horses who called themselves "horse."
She had horses who called themselves "spirit,"
and kept their voices secret and to themselves.

She had horses who had no names.
She had horses who had books of names.

She had some horses.

She had horses who whispered in the dark,
who were afraid to speak.
She had horses who screamed out of fear
of the silence, who carried knives
to protect themselves from ghosts.
She had horses who waited for destruction.
She had horses who waited for resurrection.

She had some horses.

She had horses who got down on their knees
for any saviour.
She had horses who thought their high price
had saved them.
She had horses who tried to save her, who
climbed in her bed at night
and prayed as they raped her.

She had some horses.

She had some horses she loved.
She had some horses she hated.

These were the same horses.

❧ The Friday Before ❧ The Long Weekend

～1983～

You come in here
drunk child
pour your beer
down the drain,
"apple juice,"
bullshit.
I can see you,
I can see
you, what you
are doing to yourself
is something
I can't sing about.
I can point
to the piss yellow
drops in the sink.
I can see the stagger
in your eyes
glasses askew
your voice loud
cawing
uncertain bravado
and you come in here
to be taught
to take writing
but hell,

what can I teach you
what can I do?
Something shaky and terrible
starts in my belly.
The sour reality rolls over
in my throat.
I can't do anything
but talk to the wind,
to the moon
but cry out goddamn goddamn
to stones
and to other deathless voices
that I hope will carry
us all through.

Seven series of good books for all readers:

WRITERS' VOICES
Selections from the works of America's finest and most popular writers, along with background information, maps, and other supplementary materials. Authors include: Kareem Abdul-Jabbar • Maya Angelou • Bill Cosby • Alex Haley • Stephen King • Loretta Lynn • Larry McMurtry • Amy Tan • Anne Tyler • Abigail Van Buren • Alice Walker • Tom Wolfe, and many others.

NEW WRITERS' VOICES
Anthologies and individual narratives by adult learners. A wide range of topics includes home and family, prison life, and meeting challenges. Many titles contain photographs or illustrations.

OURWORLD
Selections from the works of well-known science writers, along with related articles and illustrations. Authors include David Attenborough and Carl Sagan.

FOR YOUR INFORMATION
Clearly written and illustrated works on important self-help topics. Subjects include: Eating Right • Managing Stress • Getting Fit • About AIDS • Getting Good Health Care, among others.

TIMELESS TALES
Classic myths, legends, folk tales, and other stories from around the world, with special illustrations.

SPORTS
Fact-filled books on baseball, football, basketball, and boxing, with lots of action photos. With read-along tapes narrated by Phil Rizzuto, Frank Gifford, Dick Vitale, and Sean O'Grady.

SULLY GOMEZ MYSTERIES
Fast-paced detective series starring Sully Gomez and the streets of Los Angeles.

WRITE FOR OUR FREE COMPLETE CATALOG:

SIGNAL HILL

Signal Hill Publications
P.O. Box 131
Syracuse, NY 13210-0131